READING AND WRITING WORKSHOPS EDITION

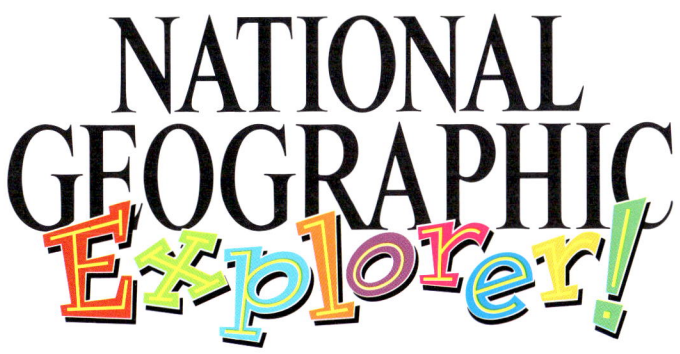

CONTENTS

2	Chew on This!
8	Life in a Deep Freeze
12	Freaky Frogs
18	King Tut
24	Concept Check

Chew

The history and science of gum around the world

By Adele Conover

on This!

Humans have been chewing gum for thousands of years. The first pieces of gum weren't much like the smooth sticks you sink your teeth into today. Sometimes they were hunks of resin, a gooey, sap-like substance that comes from trees. Other times they were gobs of latex (LAY tex). Latex is a tree substance that starts out milky, but hardens when exposed to air.

Many ancient people also tried chewing grasses, leaves, and grains. But they liked chomping on resin and latex better.

In 1993, scientists found the oldest known piece of gum in Sweden. It is a 9,000-year-old wad of resin that was sweetened with honey. Tooth marks are still in it!

Gum has stuck around a long time. As you will find out in this article, it has also covered much of the globe.

Pop-ular Purchase.
Kids in North America spend almost half a billion dollars on gum every year.

Gum Covers the Globe

About 2,000 years ago, the ancient Greeks chewed mastiche (mas TEE ka) gum. Mastiche is a yellow resin taken from the bark of the mastic tree. The Greeks thought that chewing mastiche cleaned their teeth and improved their breath.

About this time in Central America, the Maya (MY uh) Indians chomped on chicle (CHEEK lay). Chicle is a milky latex the Maya collected from a tree called the sapodilla (sap oh DEE ya). Like other natural latex, chicle becomes thick and gummy when it comes in contact with the air. The Maya chewed chicle to help their digestion and quench their thirst on long journeys.

North America Goes for Gum

Early North American Indians, including the Wampanoag (wam pa NO ag) of New England, chewed a resin gum made from spruce trees. To make the gum, the Wampanoag cut into the side of a spruce tree. The tree produced a gooey resin to patch up the cut. When the resin

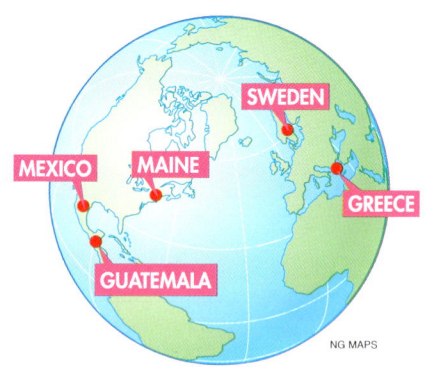

hardened, the Wampanoag scraped it off and chewed it.

Like the Maya, the Wampanoag chewed the gum to quench their thirst. Around 1700, they introduced English settlers to spruce gum. The settlers really liked chewing gum.

Sweet Successes

In 1848, a young lumberjack from Maine named John Curtis decided to mix a batch of spruce gum and sell it. He sweetened it with cornstarch and cut it into strips. He sold two strips of gum for a penny and earned $5,000 his first year. That's equal to earning about $90,000 today. In 1852, Curtis opened the world's first chewing gum factory in Portland, Maine. Spruce gum was probably the first gum to be made and sold in the United States.

In 1869, New York inventor Thomas Adams bought a large

amount of chicle. He thought he could turn the chicle into a low-priced rubber substitute for making items like balls and tires. But he couldn't get the chicle to bounce. So he decided to use his chicle to make gum. This gum tasted better than spruce gum, especially after adding sugar and flavorings like vanilla, mint, and licorice.

The most successful maker of chicle gum was William Wrigley, Jr. In 1893, he introduced two flavors that are still around today: Wrigley's Spearmint and Juicy Fruit. Adding good flavor to gum wasn't the only thing that made Wrigley successful. He was a clever businessperson. In 1915, Wrigley sent a free stick of gum to everyone listed in a United States phone book. That stunt, and others like it, made sales of gum soar.

Blown Away

Thirty-five years later, Walter Diemer invented a gum that chewers could blow into big bubbles. He called it Dubble Bubble.

Diemer's gum wasn't pretty, so he decided to add color to it. The only food coloring he had was pink. So he threw the pink coloring into the batch, and the color stuck!

Final Stretch

In the late 1940s, most chewing gum companies stopped using chicle in their gum bases. Instead, they used materials that were stretchier and easier to get. These included various types of wax, plastic, and rubber. Almost 50 years later, gum base is still made with these products.

Wrigley company in the 1890s

Factories make most gum by using wax, plastic, or rubber as the main ingredient. But in Nohbec (NO bec), a rain forest in Mexico, people do things the old-fashioned way. Workers called *chicleros* (chee CLAR os) tap trees to collect a milky substance known as *chicle* (CHEEK lay). They turn the chicle into a product they call Jungle Gum.

1 He's a Cutup.
A chiclero slashes the trunk of a sapodilla tree.

2 Ooze on Down.
A milky substance called chicle oozes down the trunk.

3 What a Strain!
Chicleros pour the chicle through a strainer to filter out dirt.

4 Strrretch!
The batch is done when it's as stretchy and sticky as taffy.

5 Pressing Work.
Chicleros shove the warm chicle into wooden boxes.

6 Ready to Go!
These 25-pound blocks will go to a factory, where workers will add flavorings and cut the gum into pieces.

Stuck on Gum

Today, men, women, and children in the United States chew an average of 300 pieces of gum a year. That can leave more than 83 billion pieces of ABC (already been chewed) gum around to gum things up! It can end up on your shoes, under your desk, in your hair, on the sidewalk, and even at the bottom of a swimming pool.

If you get gum on small items such as books or clothing, you can rub the gummy parts with ice. Or you can put the gummy parts in the freezer until they're hard. Then you can chip off the frozen gum.

Removing gum from large areas is a lot harder. Many U.S. cities are now hiring a company called GumBusters to remove gum from their sidewalks and subways. The company's 70-pound GumBuster machine uses 300°F steam to soften the gum. Next, it splashes top-secret "gumfighter" chemicals on it. Using a wire brush, it then rubs the gum until it dissolves. This service works, but it can cost up to $1,220 a day.

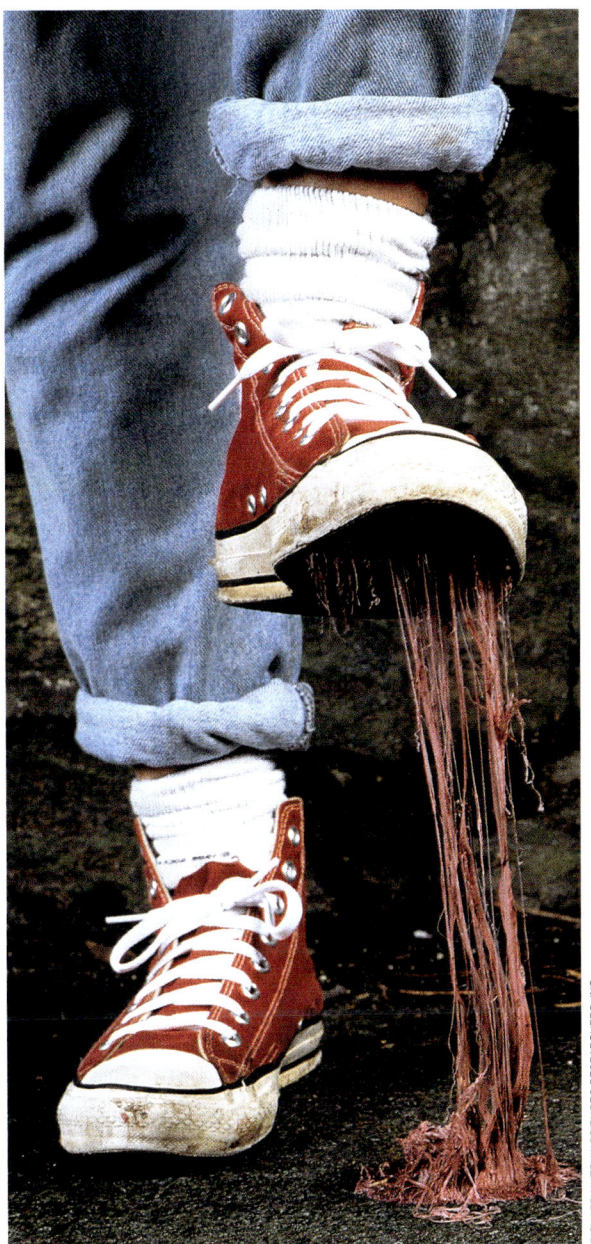

Watch Your Step!
Americans chew 83 billion pieces of gum a year. Sometimes the leftovers can be a pain in the foot.

LIFE IN A DEEP Freeze

How do animals survive the Arctic's c-c-cold winters?

BY SANDRA MARKLE

A Cool Crowd. *Walruses spend most of their time in water. Yet they rest and have babies on huge chunks of floating ice.*

Snow and ice cover the ground. Strong winds blow. The air is freezing cold. It is winter in the Arctic.

Where is the Arctic? Look at the map. The Arctic is all the land and water inside the red circle. It includes the North Pole.

The Arctic is always cold. Its **tundra,** or flat land, stays frozen all year. Yet many animals live here. They have ways to stay warm—and alive.

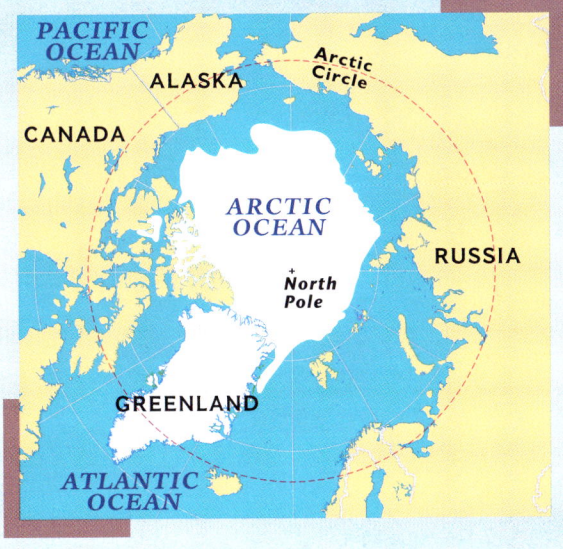

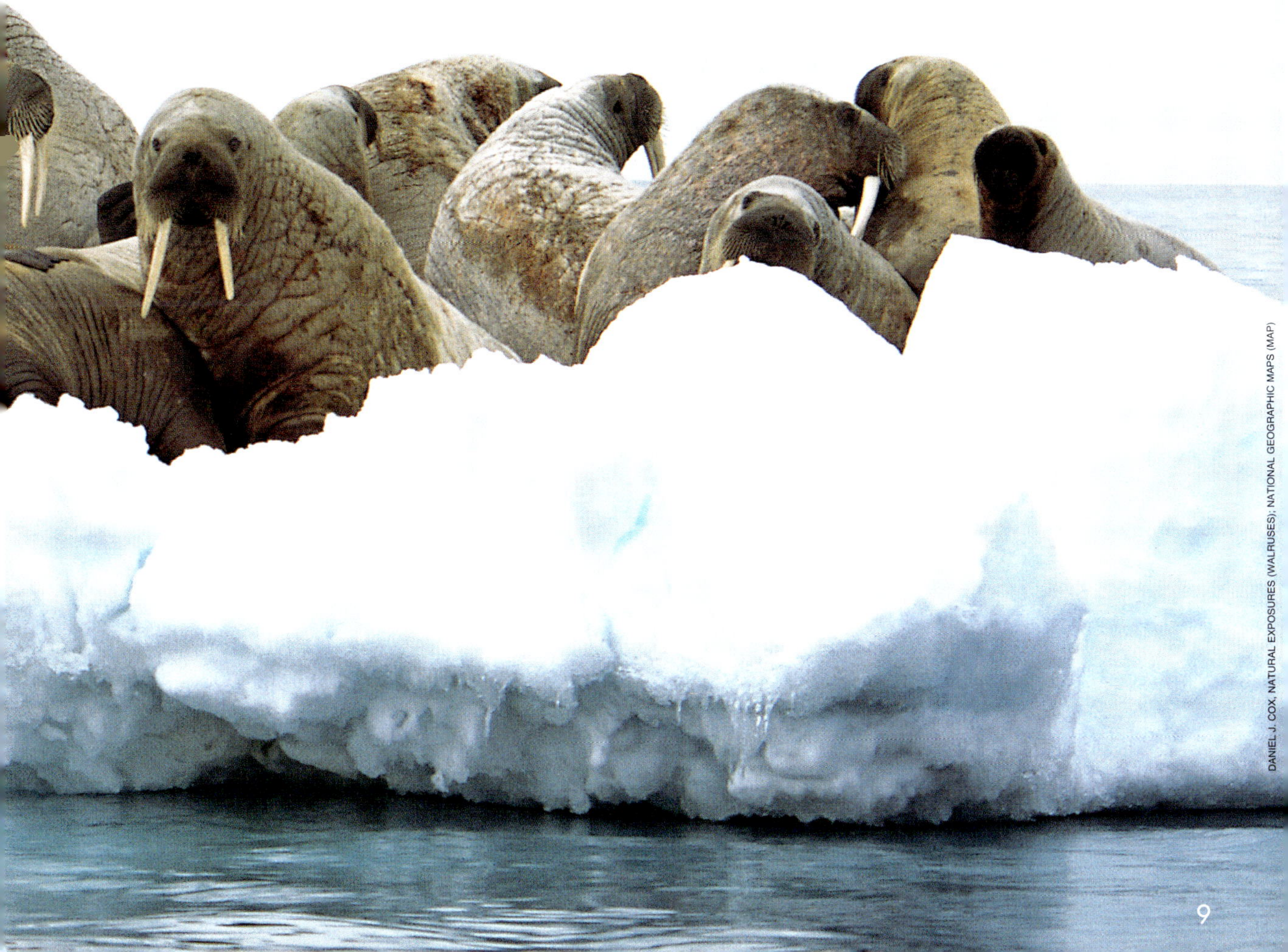

DANIEL J. COX, NATURAL EXPOSURES (WALRUSES); NATIONAL GEOGRAPHIC MAPS (MAP)

Snow Baby. *Most grizzly bear cubs are born while their mothers hibernate.*

Big Teeth. *Walruses grow long tusks, or teeth. Some are 30 inches long!*

Sleepy Winters

Some animals are not bothered by the cold. They sleep all winter. That is what grizzly bears do.

Grizzly Bear The grizzly bear eats a lot in spring, summer, and fall. It gets fat. Then winter comes. The grizzly bear **hibernates,** or sleeps deeply. The bear does not eat again until spring. It lives off its stored fat.

The Layered Look

In winter, the Arctic Ocean is covered with ice. Yet some animals hunt in the water. Fat keeps them warm.

Walrus This animal spends most of its time in cold ocean water. It dives to the ocean floor. It digs for clams.

How does a walrus stay warm? It has a thick layer of **blubber,** or fat. The fat holds in heat.

Harp Seal Harp seals also have a layer of blubber. The blubber helps them stay warm in icy water.

Harp seals are expert swimmers. They are fast in the water. They race after fish. They can stay underwater for 30 minutes at a time. Without their blubber, they would freeze!

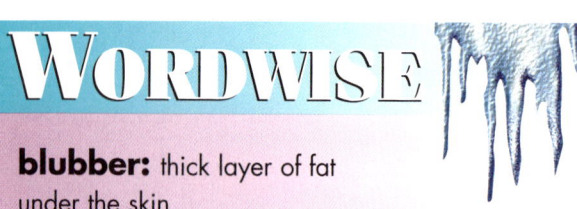

WORDWISE

blubber: thick layer of fat under the skin

hibernate: to sleep deeply for months

tundra: flat area without trees where the ground stays frozen all year

Safety in Numbers. *Muskoxen live in groups. They form a line when danger is near. This helps them stay safe.*

Dressed for Winter

In winter, many Arctic animals grow a thick coat, or layer of fur. The coats keep them safe and warm.

Muskox The muskox is always covered with shaggy hair. In winter, woolly fur grows under the shaggy hair. This thick fur coat keeps the muskox warm.

Arctic Fox The arctic fox changes color with the seasons. In summer, it has brown fur. In winter, it grows white fur. Its white coat lets the fox blend in with the snow. This helps the fox stay safe from hungry animals.

Wearing White

Some animals do not change color in winter. They wear white all year. Their color helps them hide in the snow.

Arctic Hare Some arctic hares live in the far north. The snow never melts. These hares have white fur all year. This keeps them safe. Hungry animals have a hard time seeing them.

Snowy owl

Snowy Owl Snowy owls are white birds. They blend in with the snow. These birds have two layers of feathers. The thick feathers keep them warm.

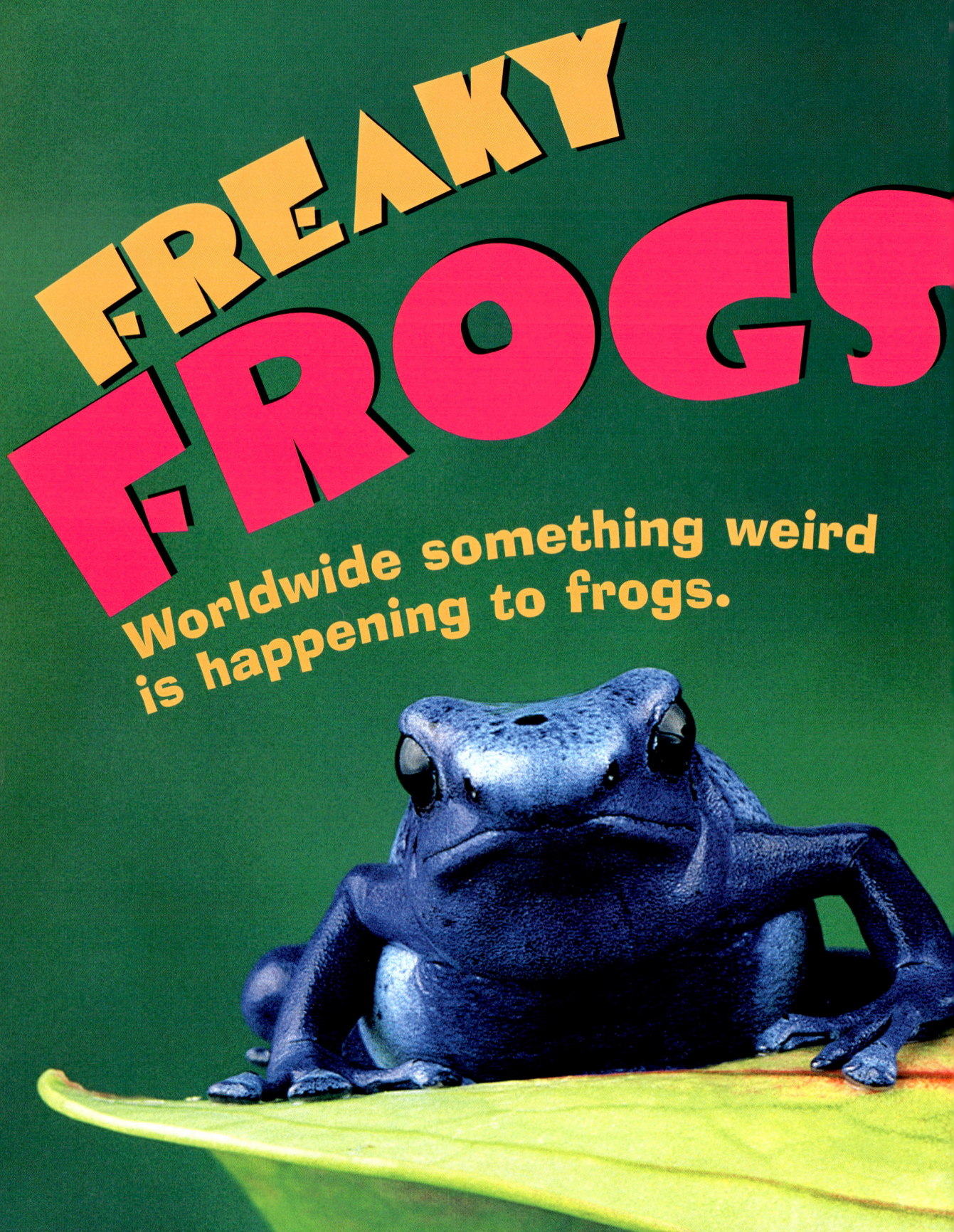

FREAKY FROGS

Worldwide something weird is happening to frogs.

By Dan and Michele Hogan

There is good news and bad news about frogs. First the good news. Scientists are finding new kinds, or **species**, of frogs.

For example, one kind looks like it is made of glass. You can see through it!

Now for the bad news. Many species of frogs are dying out. Other frogs do not look right. They are growing strange features.

Scientists want to know what is happening to these frogs. Let's find out what they know so far.

Blue poison frogs

Losing Their Homes

Most frogs like wet areas. They live in ponds, marshes, and rain forests.

Frogs like wet areas for many reasons. They lay their eggs in water. Their favorite foods live in water. Frogs can also hide from hungry animals by diving underwater.

Today, many of the places frogs live are drying up. People are draining swamps. When the land dries, people move in and build homes.

So, many kinds of frogs are losing their homes, or **habitats.** This could be causing them to die out.

Chemical Changes

Some people think chemicals may also harm frogs.

Rain can wash chemicals into ponds. The chemicals pollute the water. They also get inside frogs. This may hurt the frogs.

Chemicals cause some frogs to have fewer babies, or **tadpoles.** The chemicals can also make frogs weak.

Daddy Day Care. *A male frog (right) guards his young.*

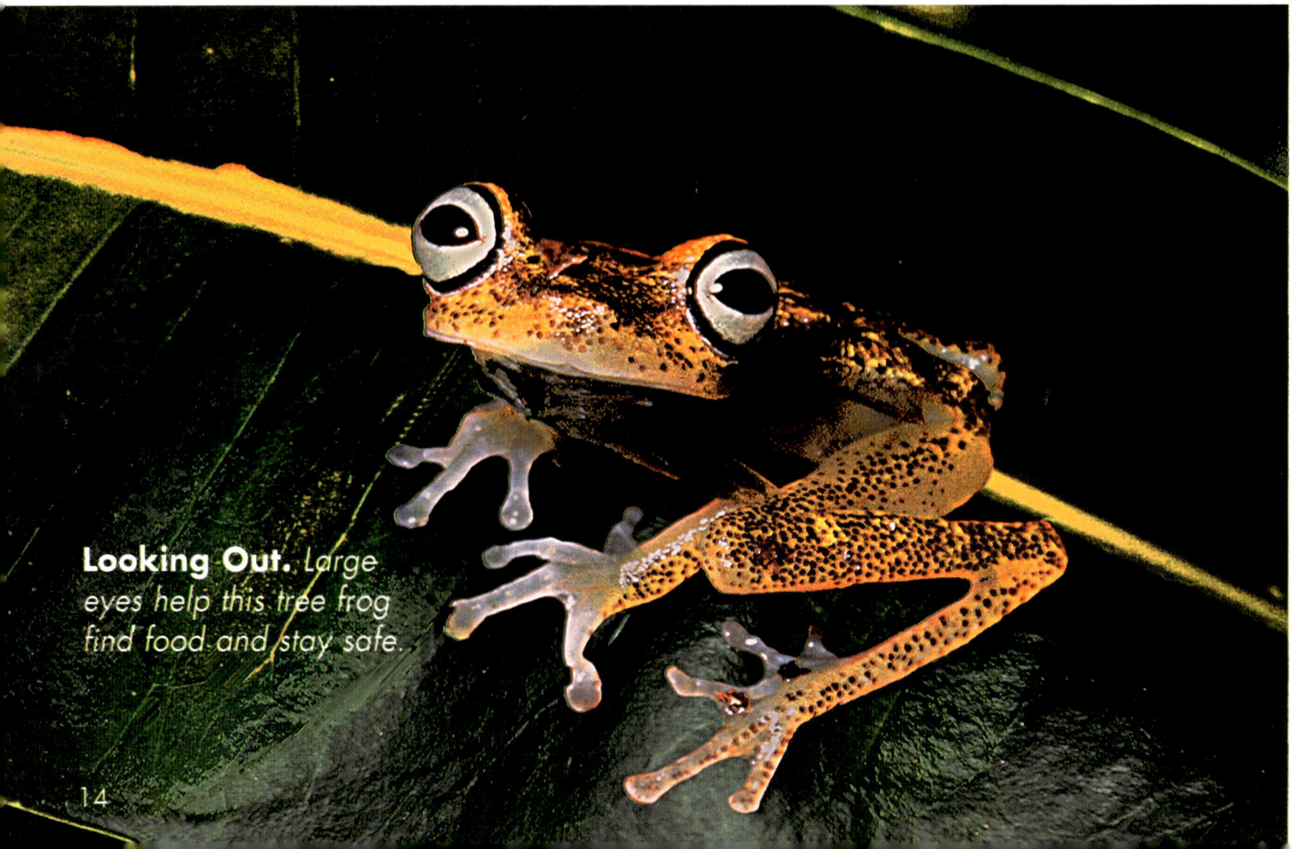

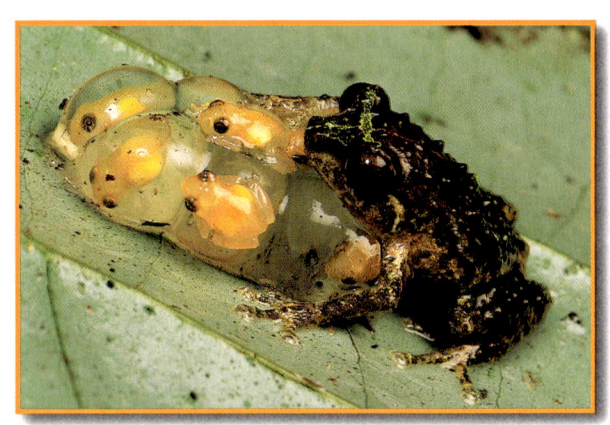

Looking Out. *Large eyes help this tree frog find food and stay safe.*

GEORGE GRALL (FROG WITH YOUNG); © RAINBOW, PICTUREQUEST (ORANGE FROG); STEVE MCCRACKEN (ARTWORK); J.H. PETE CARMICHAEL (FLYING FROG)

FAR-OUT FROGS

Smallest: The gold frog is about the size of your fingernail.

Biggest: The goliath frog can weigh as much as a house cat.

Singer: One frog sings like a bird.

Survivor: The wood frog can stay frozen for several weeks.

Java flying frog

Growing Problems

Something even weirder is going on. Many frogs have no legs. Others have too many legs, or legs in odd places.

Scientists do not know what is causing the problems. Some blame pollution or disease. Others say rays from the sun might be hurting frogs.

Jump In. *You may have seen this frog. The leopard frog is common in North America.*

Bad Frog. *This frog has too many legs. Something has caused this and other odd features.*

Dangerous Rays

Some scientists say **UV light** from the sun might be hurting frogs. UV light can harm your skin. It can cause sunburns and skin cancer.

UV light is even more harmful to frogs. It can pass through frog eggs. This might damage the eggs. When they hatch, the young frogs may have strange features.

Today, the sky does not block as much UV light as it did in the past. So UV light is a bigger problem than it used to be.

Deadly Disease

A disease might also cause the odd features. It is spread by a tiny worm. The worm lives in wetlands. The worm can give the disease to a frog. The disease can cause strange features in that frog's young.

The disease is hurting more and more frogs. Scientists want to find a way to stop the worm.

The Future of Frogs

You might think that freaky frogs are a small problem. Think again. Whatever is harming frogs might hurt other animals and people too.

Fewer frogs could also mean fewer medicines. Some kinds of frogs have **toxins,** or poisons, in their skin. Scientists use the toxins to make medicines. Without frogs, people will not have these medicines.

There is still hope for frogs. People have cleaned ponds where frogs once lived. The frogs came back!

Today, people are finding ways to save frogs. Their work may help people and other animals stay healthy too.

Green tree frogs

WORDWISE

habitat: place where a plant or animal lives
species: kind of animal or plant
tadpole: baby frog
toxin: poison
UV light: harmful rays from the sun

Big Meeting. *Scientist Zahi Hawass looks at King Tut.*

King Tut

Modern science comes face-to-face with an ancient mystery.

By Zahi Hawass
Director of Excavations at the Giza Pyramids and
the Valley of the Golden Mummies; and a
National Geographic Explorer–in–Residence

19

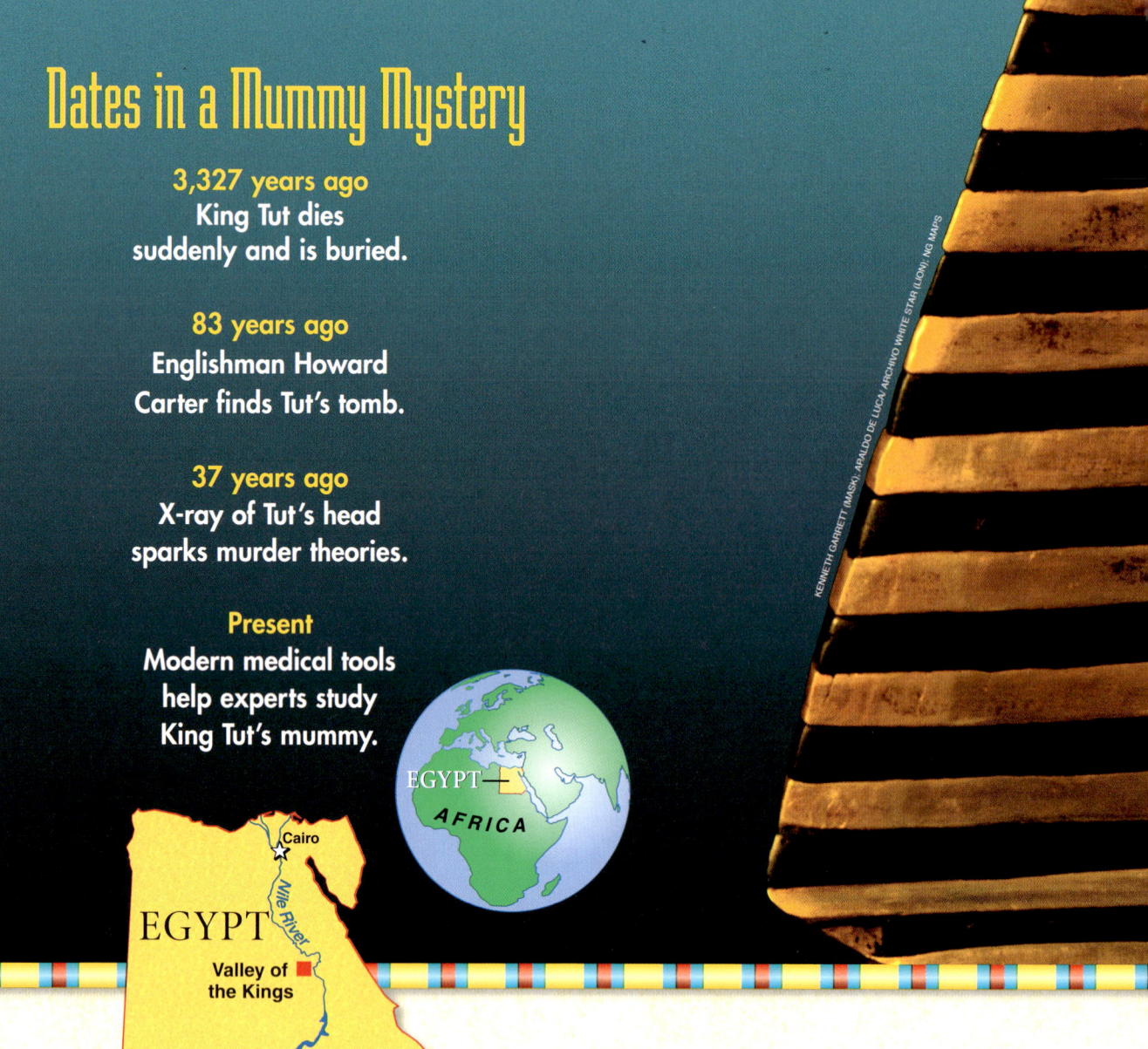

Dates in a Mummy Mystery

3,327 years ago
King Tut dies suddenly and is buried.

83 years ago
Englishman Howard Carter finds Tut's tomb.

37 years ago
X-ray of Tut's head sparks murder theories.

Present
Modern medical tools help experts study King Tut's mummy.

I felt very nervous. After all, I was taking the world's most famous **mummy** out of its tomb!

If anything went wrong, I'd be in big trouble. It could even mean the end of my career as an **archaeologist.** That's a scientist who studies the past by looking at what people left behind.

Famous Face. TOP: *This mask shows King Tut in royal clothing. It was put over his face after he died.*

Who Was King Tut?

The mummy was that of an ancient Egyptian king, or **pharaoh.** He is often called King Tut.

Much of Tut's life is a mystery. We do not even know his parents' names.

We do know that Tut was born about 3,346 years ago. He became king when he was eight or nine. He died roughly nine years later. He was buried in the Valley of the Kings.

20

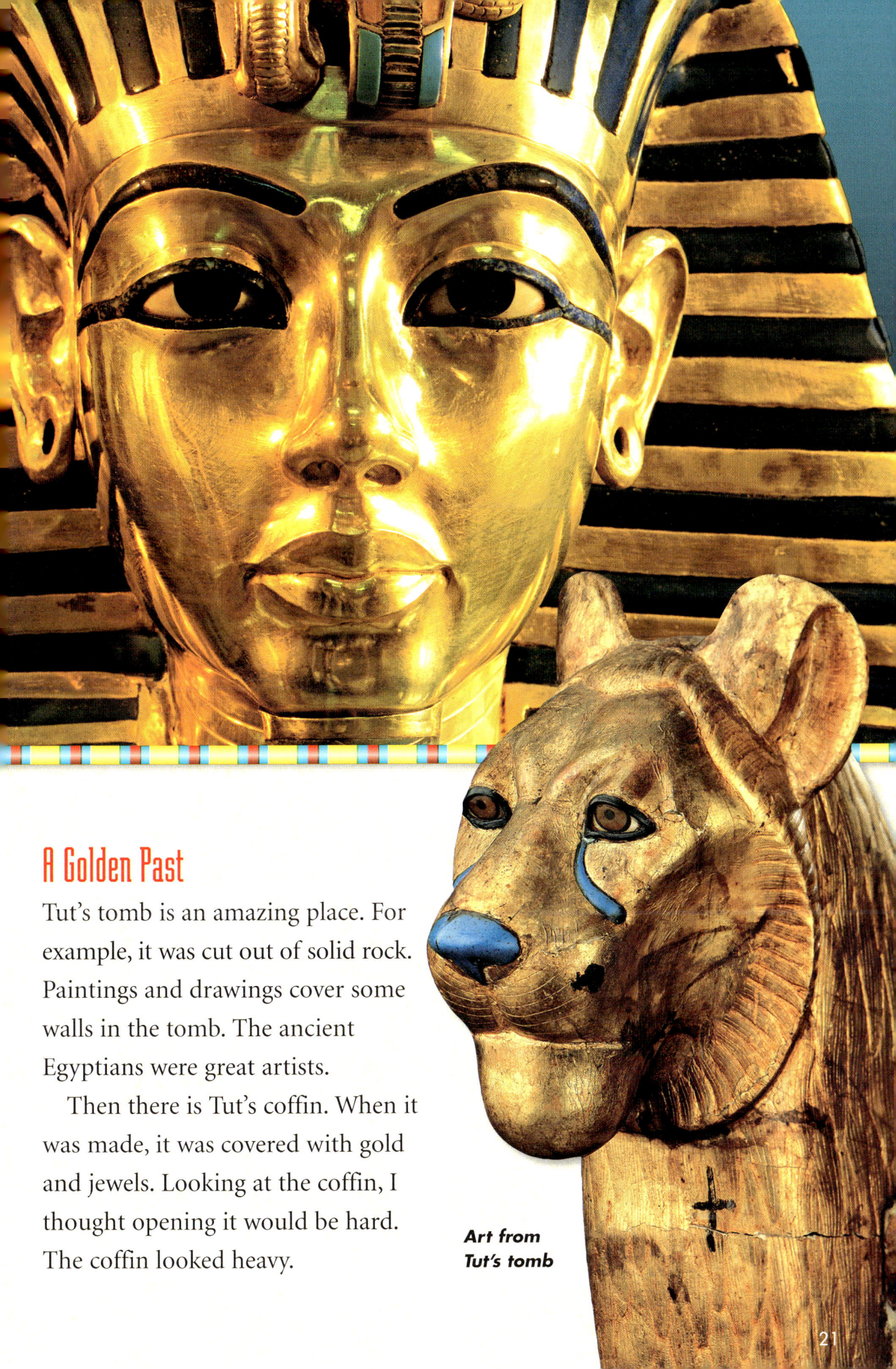

A Golden Past

Tut's tomb is an amazing place. For example, it was cut out of solid rock. Paintings and drawings cover some walls in the tomb. The ancient Egyptians were great artists.

Then there is Tut's coffin. When it was made, it was covered with gold and jewels. Looking at the coffin, I thought opening it would be hard. The coffin looked heavy.

Art from Tut's tomb

Old King, New Look. *Behind Zahi Hawass stands a CT scanner. It took 1,700 pictures of King Tut's mummy.*

High-Tech History. *Computers made this image of King Tut's head.*

Awesome Moment

I soon learned exactly how heavy the coffin is. My team used four thick ropes to lift the coffin lid. We pulled the ropes slowly and carefully.

Then came the moment to meet Tut face-to-face. I looked down. I took the cover from his head. Our faces were just inches apart.

Murder Mystery

Looking at Tut's young face and his buckteeth, I smiled. I thought of many questions I wanted to ask him. One stands out. How did Tut die?

Tut was just 19 when he died. Many people think he was killed. The mystery deepened about 30 years ago. That is when scientists took an x-ray of Tut's head.

The x-ray showed a fuzzy area at the back. Was it an injury? Had someone clubbed Tut to death?

I hoped modern medical tools might answer these questions. So we placed Tut into a **CT scanner.** It takes pictures. They show the inside of a body.

New Questions

My team used the scanner to take lots of photos. We then spent two months studying them.

We all agreed that Tut seemed fairly healthy. We also agreed that he had not been murdered. We did find one big question, however.

Tut's left leg was broken. The break may have torn the king's skin. Perhaps germs then infected the wound. That could have made Tut sick. Is that what killed him?

We may never know how Tut died. There are always mysteries to solve. We will use the CT scanner to study other mummies too. We will learn new things about Egypt's old past.

Would you like to study Egyptian mummies? Why or why not?

Wordwise

archaeologist: scientist who studies items and places from the past

CT scanner: medical tool that shows the insides of a body

mummy: body preserved by drying

pharaoh: ruler in ancient Egypt

The Face of History

What did King Tut look like? A team of scientists and artists recently tried to find out. They began by studying CT scans. Based on the pictures, the team created a model of Tut's skull.

Team members measured the skull. That helped them figure out the shape of Tut's face. An artist used the data to make the model below.

The artist had to guess at the color of Tut's skin. Modern Egyptians range from very light to quite dark. So the artist picked a shade in the middle.

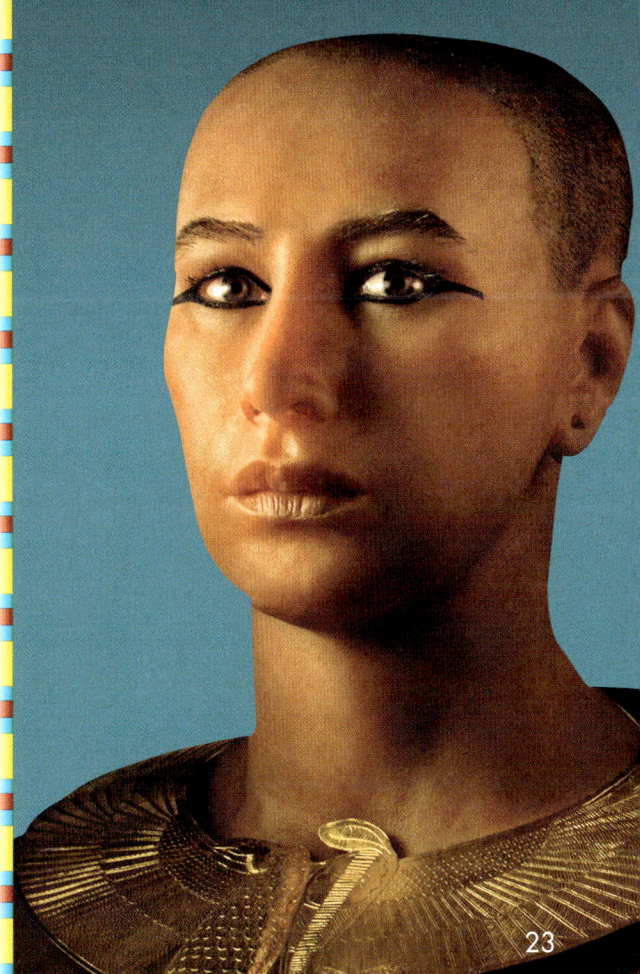

Concept Check

1. When did gum become popular? Why?

2. How do animals survive winter in the Arctic?

3. What problems are some frogs having? Why?

4. Who was King Tut? How did he die?

5. List one important idea and one fun detail from one of the articles you read.